The Rev I.M. Jolly & Friends

RIKKI FULTON

The Rev I.M. Jolly & Friends

THE VERY BEST OF LAST CALL

BLACK & WHITE PUBLISHING

First published 2004
by Black & White Publishing Ltd
99 Giles Street, Edinburgh EH6 6BZ

ISBN 1 84502 037 5

A CIP catalogue record for this book
is available from The British Library.

Cover photograph by kind
permission of BBC Scotland

CONTENTS

FOREWORD

by Gordon Menzies
Producer and Director of Scotch & Wry

Scotch & Wry began in 1978 and ended in 1993. In television comedy terms it was a glorious 15 years. *Scotch & Wry* broke all BBC Scotland audience records. With over 2 million viewers tuning in every Hogmanay we often wondered how so many Scots, including children, managed to stay up so late. The programmes were fronted, of course, by the incomparable Rikki Fulton, star of stage, screen and radio and, arguably, the greatest Scottish comedian of all time.

Rikki was also a superlative actor and writer, starring in stage plays, pantomime, television dramas and films. Indeed, when the film *Gorky Park* was shown in Scottish cinemas in the 1980s *Scotch & Wry* by then was hugely popular. When Rikki first appeared in that film, in the very serious role of a sinister KGB agent, Scottish cinema audiences burst out laughing. They just found it difficult to take him seriously.

The two leg-ends of all *Scotch & Wry* programmes were Supercop and Last Call. And both Supercop and the Rev I.M. Jolly quickly dropped the hyphen and became legends. When *Scotch & Wry* started in 1978 the idea of including a Last Call monologue came from the then up-and-coming writer, John Byrne. John had worked in the design department at Scottish Television and had witnessed at first hand many of STV's *Late Call*s. As one of the writers asked to contribute to the budding *Scotch & Wry* series, John submitted a *Late Call* by the Rev Angus McKnocker. We, in the BBC, renamed it *Last Call* and put it in the hands of our new television star, Rikki Fulton.

Prior to the beginning of *Scotch & Wry* I had first worked with Rikki in 1977 when I produced *The Scotched Earth Show*. It was a time when prospects of devolution and nationalism were high on the Scottish political agenda. The show ended with Rikki, in the guise of a Glesca Cooncillor, addressing the nation as the first Prime Minister of Scotland. Even in rehearsal the whole production team had tears of laughter running down their cheeks and we all realised that we had found the master of the television monologue.

It is widely recognised that comedy is the biggest minefield in television. No matter how imaginative the concept, how creative the production, how talented the performers, the bedrock of the programme is the script. And in our *Last Call*s we were also fortunate in that what John Byrne had started Rikki Fulton took over. Even before we started working together Rikki had established a great reputation as a stage writer. His fireside chats to his television audience as the forlorn, deadbeat Scottish minister, the Rev I.M. Jolly, are testament to his writing ability.

The story of how the name I.M. Jolly came

about is worth retelling. Rikki had submitted a *Last Call* featuring this sad, depressed Presbyterian minister but we didn't know what to call him. When I was in BBC Scotland's wardrobe department discussing costumes for that week's show, I mentioned our desperate search for a name for the gloomy minister. A dresser, who was sewing and listening – I think her name was Ruth – piped up and said, 'how about Jolly?' I immediately phoned Rikki and the Rev I.M. Jolly was born.

Although we featured various other men of the cloth (and even a lady) in our early series of *Scotch & Wry*, once we moved to annual Hogmanay specials there was only one candidate for the *Last Call* spot – the Rev I.M. Jolly. And so all the later *Last Call*s (nos 9-24) are by Jolly aka Rikki Fulton. Although Rikki wrote the Jolly *Last Call*s, he always welcomed ideas from other writers who contributed to *Scotch & Wry*. Over the years script editors working on the series always made constructive suggestions and script writers, such as

Donnie Kerr, offered interesting lines of thought which Rikki was only too happy to explore.

It's been a pleasure reading through the scripts again and it helps if you can also visualise Rikki's delivery with his little smiles, knowing glances and, of course, the famous Fulton pauses for maximum effect. I hope that you enjoy reliving your favourite *Last Call* moments as much as I have.

1

THE KNICKER-KNOCKING VICAR

𝔯𝔢𝔟 𝔞𝔫𝔤𝔲𝔰 𝔐𝔠𝔎𝔫𝔬𝔠𝔨𝔢𝔯

Ah . . . good evening. I was cleaning out the wife's saddlebag the other night when I came across an old *News of the World*, the headline of which caught my eye. It read 'Knackered Knicker-Knocking Vicar Knicked', which reminded me of a story I heard while I was a padre in the Pioneer Corps. It seems there were these two nuns who . . . Self-sacrifice is my theme tonight. Self-sacrifice, my dear brethren, is what all of us – all of you – should be at like knives this weather . . . not just because it's Lent, 'cos of course you never get it back, and not just because it makes us all feel a lot better. No . . . what we . . . or rather you, should be doing, is cutting down on those little luxuries that all of us enjoy – like a light bulb in the lavatory and cheese in the mousetrap . . . sod the mice, let them do without like the rest of us . . . and with the money we . . . or rather you, save . . . we . . . you . . . should invest in several tins of white paint, the significance of which shall become abundantly clear as my little sermonette progresses. Yes . . . hmm . . . humm?

Oh, yes . . . let us take a look at the parable of the Prodigal Son, for is there not a lesson for us all to be found in that story? Of course there is . . . remember how it goes? It came to pass in the land of Judea that a Prodigal did set off in search of the world. And he did go into the world and eat the fruits of the world and yet one day he said to himself, haw Jimmy – for such was his name . . . Jimmy Such . . . 'It's a funny old world, I think I'll go and visit the old man.' And he did set off to visit his Father who was a long way off.

Meanwhile, back at the farm, there was

another son who was not the Prodigal and he was called Mug, on account of his staying home and running the father's farm, and going the messages and getting the coal in and all that. And it came to pass that Mug, for it was he, took it upon himself to ask his father why the Prodigal had been given all the family savings, the bike and a big load of sausage rolls and been sent off to enjoy the fruits of the world and his father replied saying, how was he to know but that was how it was in those days and that was why he, Mug, was so-called, and would he kindly shut his face and would he bring in another pail of coal as the fire was going down . . . ?

And it came to pass that in time the Prodigal did return to his father's house and his father upon seeing him fell upon his neck, saying 'I must get that step repaired,' and did kiss him.

'Will you not stop falling upon my neck and kissing me, the neighbours are looking at us funny, father. Also I do believe the chap with the coal bucket is getting angry.' And his father did chastise the elder son and exhorted him to run to the butcher's before it was shut and get a fatted calf or half a pound of mince or a Chinese carry-out that they might feast and be merry for the Prodigal was gone and was returned. And the elder son, whose name was Mug, did discover within himself a terrible rage and did give vent to that wrath, and kicked the dog. And his father did upbraid him mightily which suited him quite well, and said unto him, 'This is my son who went and was gone, and he has went and come back again.' And the elder son, Mug, for it was he, turned his face unto the Prodigal and thought for a time and then said, 'Where is the bike?' And there was great feasting and drinking in the father's house that night and for many nights there-after.

We can all learn something from that simple story, don't you think? And just before I go don't forget to go out with those little pots of paint and write up on every available space, 'The Reverend McKnocker is Innocent' – OK?

I never nicked those knickers!

Warder comes on and leads him off, with his baggy pink drawers.

I'm innocent, I tell you! Those weren't my knickers . . .

2

A DAMP DISGRACE

𝔉ather 𝔗homas 𝔇ooley

Good evening. You'll remember what it says in Genesis Chapter Seven . . . (for I'm sure you've only this minute put the book down) . . . 'In the six hundredth year of Noah's life' . . . he woulda done well if the Pension Scheme had been goin' then, wouldn't he? . . . 'in the second month, the seventeenth day of the month, the same day were all the fountains of the great deep broken up and the windows of heaven were opened . . . And the rain was upon the earth forty days and forty nights.' That's not all that different from some of the weather we've been having lately. In fact, by comparison with some of our Scottish weather, Noah was having something of a DRY spell.

I was reminded of this during a particularly wet spell earlier this year. I was having a chinwag in the church hall with some of my parishioners during a break in the bingo, when Michael, a young fellow in his forties, swam over to have a word with me.

'Father,' says he, takin' off his Crombie and wringin' it out into a fire bucket. 'D'you not think it about time we had a ROOF on this place?'

'Ah, Michael, my son,' says I, helpin' Mrs Doyle into the rowing boat, 'you've noticed!'

'Father,' says he, 'it's a damp disgrace!'

While upbraiding him for his use of strong language in front of the nursing mothers, I couldn't help but congratulate him on the pun.

'Michael,' says I, 'disgrace it certainly is – and DAMP it most certainly is. But, worse than that, have you any idea how foolish we feel playin' bingo sittin' waist-deep in water.'

Michael concurred. I think mebbe he'd been eatin' somethin'. I leaned back on the oars and fixed him with a challengin' stare. 'Michael,'

says I, givin' Mrs Doyle a hand with the baling
. . . 'Michael, I've got the League of the Cross
and the Children of Mary workin' night and
day, but sure they won't be gettin' the roof
itself before Ash Wednesday, and then it's Lent,
– so we've no hope of gettin' it back before
Christmas.'

'Ah, Father,' says he, 'I'm thinkin' that might
be just a bit tardy. Sure I know they're workin'
flat out, but I had in mind something a bit
more expedient . . .'

'Ah,' says I, tryin' desperately to grasp his
meaning *and* Mrs Doyle's hand, for she'd
slipped over the side, 'Now what would you
be gettin' at, my son?'

'Well,' says he, climbin' onto the table that
was floatin' past. 'Ye know the Ark you've
been buildin' in the vestry?'

'I do,' says I, for I did.

'Don't you think,' says he, slidin' off the
table and takin' old Mr Crouch and six of the
Doyles with him.

'Don't you . . . how about we turned the

damn thing and stuck it on top of the Hall.
The Knights of St Columba are a stout body
of men. They could get the thing into position
between now and Vespers.'

'Ah, Michael,' says I, tryin' desperately to
prevent the skiff over-turning and pitchin'
meself and Mrs Doyle into the murky waters.
'Ah, Michael, me son, that's easier said than
done . . . and anyways, if it's the carpet you're
worried about, the Legion of St Mary and the
St. Vincent de Pauls can have that up and dried
off over the boiler in no time at all.'

'It's not just the carpet,' says he, as he came
up for the third time, 'when it gets this clammy,
the bingo cards get a wee bit soggy and we
can't read the numbers.'

'Ah, well, Michael,' says I, 'in that case I can
see it's a matter of real urgency. I'll attend to
it just as soon as I've given Mrs Doyle here the
kiss of life.'

Good night.

3

LOVELY WATTER THIS

Rev David Goodchild

Floor manager comes into shot and arranges a vase, a water carafe and tumbler, bible, etc on a desk in the Last Call set. Looking furtively in all directions, he produces a bottle of gin and takes a swig.

Hearing someone approaching, he up-ends the bottle in the water carafe and stands in front shielding it as the producer walks past.

Producer: Alright, Alex?
FM: Er . . . yes, Gordon. All set.
Producer: OK. Fine. This'll be a take. Get the old buzzard in.

The producer walks out of shot.

The FM takes the gin bottle out of the carafe and stuffs it back whence it came, as the minister approaches.

FM: Alright, Reverend? Just sit there. OK? This is your first time, isn't it?
Minister: Yes. I hope it'll be all right.
FM: It'll be great, don't worry. Relax and wait for my signal.

FM goes out of shot. Minister clears his throat nervously, then pours himself a glass of water and drains the glass. His eyes widen in mild surprise as the gin hits his stomach. He braces himself and waits to begin.

    The FM gives him a signal and the Last Call music begins.

Good evening. Each night this week I shall have the pleasure of coming into your homes and chatting to you about normal everyday things. (*He burps.*) Excuse me – things which, as we know only too well, sometimes turn out to be anything but normal *(another rift blows his cheeks out)*, and certainly don't happen every day.

He clears his throat and pours himself another glass of water, takes a mouthful and does a slight double-take of pleasant surprise.

I'm thinking, when I say that of 'The Good Samaritan'. Now – 'There was a man' – if you'll pardon the John Cairney – who had no idea when he got up that morning that he was going to go down in history. As it happens he failed his geography and physics as well, but that's another story. You'll remember what Deuteronomy said to Leviticus about Exodus . . . er . . .

He can't remember, so takes another swig.

. . . so there's no point in bringing it up again. *(Burps.)* Excuse me. Now, most of us, at one time or another, have had the opportunity . . .

of being a good Samaritan at one time or
another without perhaps being . . . er . . .
aware of it.

He pours another glassful and sips.

Let me tell you about Jim and Elsie. That's not
their real names, of course, but we'll call them
Jim and Elsie in order to . . . er . . . protect the
innocent. Ha-ha . . . protect the . . . ha-ha . . .
who loves ya baby! Now I first knew Jim . . .

Drinks and repours.

(Sings) It MUST be Jim . . . an ordinary guy . . .
er . . . when I first knew Jim he was a happy-
go-lucky devil-may-care . . . don't-give-a . . .
for instance . . .

Another sip.

. . . and if he had a stiff with El . . . if he had
a TIFF with Elsie . . . s'lovely water this –

where d'you get your water? Elsie would always say to Jim . . . Course that wasn't their real names . . . everybody knew their REAL names. It was wee Sammy Dunn and his wife Nirvanah, wasn't it. Nirvanah. Known as Nivir-nivir for short. Nivir-nivir done talking . . . Nivir done borrowin' . . . Nivir let ye have a . . . Oh, we all KNEW her . . . I mean were ACQUAINTED with HER.

Now pouring and supping continuously.

Anyway, Sammy began to change . . . Ah don't mean like Jekyll and Hyde . . . it was just . . . well, one day he'd be Sulky and Moody and the next he'd be Morecambe and Wise, know what Ah mean.

He takes another large swig.

And it soon became clear that he wis on the booze. Well, Ah tried tae do whit Ah could. So Ah got him tae get in touch wi' Alcoponics

Analogous . . . 'cos he wis quite clearly a
Archipelago . . . s'marvellous watter this . . .
where d'ye go tae get this watter . . . listen . . .
ha-ha . . . Ah think Ah'll get in touch with the
Altiseptics Eponymous masel' . . . TAE
RESIGN.

Anyway, this night Big Nirvanah 'n' me goes
home tae find Wee Sammy onny flerr absovery
comblooteratit . . . an' the bath running . . .
Aye . . . watter runnin' doon the sterr – oot
the close mooth . . . ye've never seen sae much
watter . . . no as good as ssiss watter, mind ye
. . . but watter everywhere . . . rushing –
pouring – streamin . . .

Here, would you excuse me a minute . . . Ah
feel a prayer comin' on. Ah'll be back in a
minute . . . keep ma place.

He gets up and leaves the set.

Excuse me, where's the lavatory? Excuse me,
sir, is there a lavvy in the house . . . ?

4

SODOM AND GOMORRAH

Rev A. King Bones

Production Assistant: Pssssst! Pssssst!
Rev. comes to with a start.
Rev: Mmmmmmm?
PA: Pssssssst!
Rev: Who is? I just dozed off for a m . . .
PA: Good evening.
Rev: Pardon?
PA: Good evening.
Rev: (*Pleasantly to the PA*) Oh, good evening.
PA: Not to ME – to THEM!
Rev: Oh, have we started?*(To camera)* Good evening. During the . . . er . . . for the next few mon . . . er . . . wee er . . . days . . . evenings . . . oh! (*He stops abruptly and looks around, obviously waiting.*)

PA: Why did you stop?

Rev: A red light came on.

PA: The red light is always on. *(To his producer)* What? Yes. *(To studio)* I'm sorry – CUT!

The screen goes blank.

Rev: I'm awfully sorry. Should I not have stopped there? I haven't broken anything, have I?

PA: Not at all. Just take your opening position, please. Stand by.

Sig. music and lights. Rev. is asleep again.

PA: Psssssssst!

Rev: *(Jerking awake)* So – until we meet again. Goodnight.

PA: From the beginning!

Rev A. King Bones, defiantly:

Good evening! From the beginning . . . er . . . there was darkness, you see. There was darkness everywhere. Everywhere in the world there was darkness except for that wee red light there. And you know, friends, we're still in – er – still in the . . . and what are they doing about it? Look at our young people – what are they doing for – for – er . . . what sort of life . . . WAFFLE. That's all they do . . . waffle. Waffle, waffle – my God it's a long time since I tasted . . . Mind you they think they're everybody – the young ones – and they're not – they're only some of us . . . but they seem to think – and how many times – when did you – you've seen it yourself. Arrogant and – and – half of them can't put two sentences together. A young fella challenged me the other day. He said, 'What would you do about Gomorrah and that other place if the people were alive today?' Sodam, I said. That's – er – what the other place was called. Sodam and Gomorrah. I mean, we've all heard the old song 'How are things in er – er –' But there IS a way.

And those of us who are that way inclined – er – inclined in that w – er – pointing in that direction – er – must be prepared to stand up and SAY – er – what we're doing standing there. 'Cos you know as well as I do – when there – and there are so many of the . . . Just the other . . . Let me put it another way.

One day when I was a very small – er – er – what d'you call it – er – BOY. I was a small boy. I was playing golf with my father. And he hit his ball off the tee at the – er – you know the hole that has a dog leg to the . . . doesn't matter. His ball ended up right behind a tree. So my father got in behind the tree and he took out his . . . er . . . er . . . what was it he took out now – his mashie. That's right. It was a mashie in those days. Nowadays it's a – er – anyway. He said to me – and I'll never forget this. He said to me – er I was only a child at the time, but I've never forgotten . . . he said – er – what was it he said now . . . er . . . Yes, he said, Agnes, he said – he had a terrible memory my father, he said, life is like – er – er life is like . . . what was it he said life was like . . . I've never forgotten this . . . He said, life is like – was it a dustbin . . . Yes – I've never forgotten this . . . He said – life is like a – no, it wasn't a dustbin . . .

Lights dim and the music plays but A. King Bones is not listening.

. . . I've never forgotten. It was the – the fifth – that's right – the fifth tee and he went behind this tree . . . and he said . . . that's right – he said – I'll always remember this . . .

5

I'D BURN THE
LOT OF YEZ

Rev W. E. Free

Aye. Good evening. I just want ye tae know that it gives me no pleasure at all to be sittin' here in this den of iniquity surrounded by these imps o' Satan and whoremasters – talkin' tae a lot o' unrepentant sinners. Hedonistic hellhounds the lot o' ye – sittin' out there on yer fat bums refreshing yer private parts wi' yon Larger – that reaches the places other beers cannae reach . . . surrounded by yer wall-tae-wall carpets, yer freezers, dishwashers and electric light.

Ah'd burn the lot o' yez if Ah hud hauf a chance.

Look at yersel's – oglin' this hellish box –

this infernal invention o' Satan – gloatin' over the corruption o' *Coronation Street* – the CARNALITY o' *Crossroads* – the unrestrained sexual excesses o' *Stars on Sunday*.

(To camera left) Aye, it's YOU Ah'm talkin' to . . . Ah saw ye there huvin' another swig.

(To camera right) And here you, Missus – don't you DARE make tea while Ah'm on!

Yer a' fur hell and damnation -- the lot o' yez – except, maybe, those that kept their eyes shut 'til Ah came on.

Believe me, I am dumbfounded at the wickedness which pervades our society. Even in Ardnasheuch – oh, God, the sinners we have there. Especially the youngsters. What wi' their hair frizzed up and their make-up and their earrings and their beads roon their necks. And the lassies are just as bad.

And the DRINKING and the GAMBLIN'. I could scarce believe it when I heard that aul Tam Cauldwell had turned his byre intae a BINGO hall. Ah'm told that if it wisnae fur the smell he'd be makin' a fortune. I went up there the other night tae see fur masel' and – Oh, the shame – the disgrace – Ah won the Snowball!

The wickedness in Ardnasheuch you just wouldnae believe. Fornicatin' . . . at least two or three times a year! WIFE SWAPPIN'!!!! Ah'm told Jimmy Anderson got a second-hand bike for his only last week. Mind you, Ah can see how a good man can so easily be deflected from the paths of righteousness by the temptations of the flesh.

Take aul Sandy McCulloch – he wis our bell-ringer. And a finer bell ye never heard ring. A good man – who lived a solitary bachelor's life like masel' – worked in the fields all day – came home and made himsel' some stewed rhubarb for his supper – went tae his bed and wis up at the crack o' five in the mornin'.

Every Saturday he would buy himsel' a quarter o' mint imperials and tho' he was passionately fond o' mint imperials he widnae touch a single one til he'd rung his bells and wis settled in his pew in the Kirk.

Now it came to pass that a widow-wumman

came to live next door tae Sandy. A painted, schemin' hussy if ever I saw one. Willie first set eyes on her as she hung oot her . . . her smalls, one Monday. Oh, he wis struck by her appearance – blonde hair, painted fingernails and great big clothes-poles. Well, on the Tuesday she said hello tae him ower the back wall. Dressed in a kinna flimsy negligé she was showing everything that God gave her, and, my God, God has been generous. On Wednesday she came tae his door to borrow a cup o' sugar – didnae have a grain in the place, she said. On the Thursday she asked if he'd come in and fix her pulley – but it was HER that got up the ladder and Sandy hud tae haud it fur her. WELL – when he looked up what d'ye think he saw – YE'RE RIGHT – a TWO PUN PACKET O' SUGAR!

Then they started havin' stewed rhubarb thegither in the evenin's. Mind you, it caused a terrible stramash at five in the mornin' – fur they've only wan between them. And IT'S ootside.

On the Friday she asked him in for supper. She laid on his favourite dinner – smokies – washed down with sparkling Lucozade.

Well, it went straight tae Sandy's heid. Then the schemin' Jezebel asked him if he'd like a mint imperial and led him intae the bedroom where she kept them in a beautiful hand-carved ivory box . . . at her bedside. They lay down on the bed and she kissed him – such a kiss it was – Sandy was absolutely speechless – both his dentures hud come out. Well, she wis wearin' one o' these dresses that fastened wi' a single brooch on her shooder, and Sandy – now out of his mind with passion and desire . . . took her in his arms. His left arm went round her and his hand straight to the clasp and before she knew what he wis doin' – he wis away wi' hauf her imperials. They didnae speak all day Saturday. And then on the Sunday the brazen hussy comes up and offers tae pull his bells for him. Well, take it from me it is the end when a single man lets a wumman near his bells. Aye, and that wis his downfall.

They got theirsel's married in Glasgow for I wouldnae touch them. Well, what consideration did he huv for me – I have nae wife and wi' him gone Ah've got tae pull ma ain bells.

Oh, and as I think of them now – away there in Majorca – drinkin' and gamblin' and fornicatin' Ah can only think o' wan thing. AH WISH AH HUD HAUF HIS LUCK!

6

HOLDING ON

Father Kevan Dulally

The Last Call set – but it is empty. And the PA supervising is keeping an anxious eye open for the missing Reverend. The director appears.

Director: Have you seen Father Kevan?

PA: Is he not in make-up?

Director: No – I've just been there. Find the old fool, will you, Alex. We've to get this *Last Call* in the can and we're running out of time.

PA: Sure!

The director walks out of shot. From the other side of the studio appears Kevan Dulally.

Father: Ah, there you are, my child. I've been lookin' everywhere for you.

PA: And we for you, Father.

Father: Ah, now that's what I want to talk to

you about.

PA: What?

Father: A wee for me. I think I'll have to go before I speak to the nation.

PA: I'm sorry, Father, do it now. Time is running out.

Father: Indeed. We must.

PA: No, I'm sorry, we must get on. Please sit here. NOW! *(Pushes him into the chair.)* And stand by . . . PLEASE.

Father: *(Looking at fountain)* Do we have to have that here . . . ?

PA: Quiet – PLEASE! Quiet everyone.

Goodevenin'. I was reminded recently of the man who sat beside a stream . . . (!!!) . . . watchin' another man cast his flies upon the water – er – fishin' from the opposite bank. After some four hours the angler called over and said, 'Did you never thinkin of tryin' the fishin' yourself?'

'Oh, I'd like to,' replied the onlooker, 'but I doubt if I'd have the patience for it.'

Now it seems to me that LIFE is like that. Some people just sit around not able to do the things they so desperately want to do . . . *(crossing and uncrossing his legs)* while others just – get up and go! Last week I was visitin' a young lad who was in hospital. Apparently he had been kickin' this bladder . . . er – this football about in a field, and he'd fallen and hurted his knee. So here he was in hospital with his leg in the air havin' the water drained off . . .

Anyway as I was returnin' from the hospital I thought to meself, I'll just go and give a blessin' to my old friends the Duggans, for it had just turned ten-to-one and I knew they liked to eat at one o'clock. It was Duggan himself who opened the door.

'Hello, Father. You've got a great nose on you – the dinner's just this minute on the table.'

'Now there's a coincidence,' I said, and laughed. Coincidence my cassock. I can smell mince at five hundred yards. Now they're a lovely family, the Duggans, although life hasn't been all that easy for them. Patrick Duggan's been out of a job for over twenty years. In fact, he's been going to the Social Security that long he's convinced he works there. Indeed only last week they presented him with a gold watch. And, you know, one wonders what a man does – how he passes the time when he's been idle for so long. *(Fr. Dulally is getting more and more desperate)*. Well, when I say idle, I have to remember he has thirteen children. There's Anthony, Seumas, Michael, Anne-Marie, Marie-Anne, Rosemary, Rosemary-Anne, Rosemary-Anne-Margaret, Rosemary-Anne-Margaret-Patrick, Hymie, and two-month-old baby called Quits. At least it seems that's what Mrs Duggan called her since I understand she intends that to be her last. A thought further confirmed by the fact that she's bricked up the bedroom door.

Anyway, that's all by the way. We had a lovely meal together. But round about the puddin' I suddenly noticed that Anthony was in a kind of a trance. His eyes rolling heavenwards, his brow deeply furrowed and his lips tightly compressed. I could see he had something on his mind. 'Father,' he said suddenly. 'Why is it that priests have got to be sellotape?'

Well now, there was a question!!!

I'm afraid I don't know the answer, Anthony, I said. The only thing I can tell you is that I am stuck with it. *(Father Dullaly is still fidgetting and crossing and uncrossing his legs.)*

There was the whole basic problem of our society if only we had the wit to see it. So many of us are trapped, unable to move, although desperate to be elsewhere and doing other things.

(He is getting truly desperate now.)

We've all got problems, even me!!

The pressure – the pressure is so great we just have to give up and let nature take its course.

Somehow we grit our teeth and hold in – I mean, hold on.

We're all rushing around, looking for a place

to go. The more we can't seem to find it, the more desperate we look.

The more . . . and there's no use crossing our legs. I mean, our fingers. Luck has no place in the scheme of things.

I mean, we have to believe no matter what sort of trouble we're in, there is someone who will help. Someone who . . . *(It is too late for Father Dulally. He looks down. There is a dawning realisation – a slow smile. He looks down again, adjusts his seat and speaks)*:

You see the Lord giveth and . . . . *(Up comes the Last Call music)*

7

THE OUAGADOUGOU TRIBE

𝔐𝔯𝔰 𝔍𝔡𝔞 𝔆𝔩𝔬𝔰𝔢𝔰𝔥𝔞𝔳𝔢

Good evening. I have recently returned from
the Horn – if you'll pardon the expression –
of Africa, where Gervais – that's my husband
by marriage – and I have been missionaries
for the past twelve years or so. When we were
first married, Gervais had a little church right
up in the far north-west of Scotland, but it
was extremely cold there and my husband's
stipend was very small. So we opted to become
missionaries and I must say the warm climate
seems to suit him.

All our time in Africa has been spent living
and working among the OUAGADOUGOU
tribe. They are pygmies, you know, no more
than four feet or so high, and often I would

see them wandering naked through the long-stemmed thistledown with great broad grins on their faces . . . giggling with each other as if something had tickled their fancy.

The name of their village – Ouagadougou – comes from their own language which, roughly translated, means 'turn left at the cesspool and mind where you put your feet.' Would, alas, that we had known this that first day Gervais and I arrived at the village. As we approached the large wooden entrance gate, all the natives were gesticulating. It was probably the hot weather. Then they started waving at us and shouting 'WOOLLAMOOGA! WOOLLA-MOOGA.' Taking this to be some sort of greeting, Gervais and I hurried through the gate – and found ourselves up to here in WOOLLAMOOGA!

It was some time before the Ouagadougous ventured near us! . . . Although they very kindly offered us a little hut to sleep in – just downwind of them.

When we eventually made contact, the

witchdoctor – a charming man – taught us how to use the damsoras when entering or leaving the village through the wooden gate. The damsoras turned out to be a rather large pair of old wellies, and, incidentally, it was Gervais – ever ready with a statistic – who pointed out that the wellies were 27" high and the witchdoctor's inside leg measurement was 22. He didn't go out much. It was probably he, too, who gave them the name of damsoras.

Ah, the happy days we spent there in Ouagadougou. I taught the children to read and write some sort of basic English and Gervais ran the bingo hall and the casino. I introduced the children to two books – the bible and, for very good reasons, *Plumb It Yourself* by H.D. Ballcock. In this way they would learn to care for their brethren and at the same time – look after their cistern.

The children were marvellous. What a sense of humour they had. And such great practical jokers. I never knew from one night to the next

WHAT I would find in my bed. A snake . . . a scorpion . . . a tarantula. One night I actually found Gervais. I think the rascals must have put something in his tea. I think he was as surprised as I was.

School, of course, was always out of doors. I would wear a wide cool skirt and blouse and the boys – nothing at all.

And let me tell you I have never seen . . . we all learned a great deal from each other. And when we got thirsty I would say to the boys. 'Now – up tree, you – get coconut.' And, laughing, they'd reply, 'No up tree us – UP YOU!' And so, of course, I'd have to climb the tree and the boys would stand underneath laughing as they looked up me – up at me.

Ah, those dear boys. Some of them must be eighteen or nineteen now and I can't wait to see how they've grown.

Gervais on the other hand is not so keen to go back. He and the witchdoctor, alas, had a slight altercation on one occasion and Gervais lost his temper . . . I'm afraid he told the witchdoctor where to stick his wellies. Didn't you, dear?

(Gervais, now a midget, is sitting on the table.)

8

THE LOVELY MRS ATKINS

Rev Justin Thyme

Good evening! I was rummaging through the attic the other evening – looking, as it happened – for a clean semit – when I came across an old trunk containing some mementos of my youth . . . an old knuckleduster, a bicycle chain, a silk stocking, a suspender belt and a pair of those awful light blue celanese knickers. Oh, don't go getting the wrong idea. They were just the trophies of an entirely innocent game of strip poker!

They belonged to a wee lassie by the name of Ivy McMenemie. I'll never forget Ivy. She had the biggest set of dentures I think I've ever seen. She still lives and works in the parish. If you'd like to meet her just go into

the Co-op drapery department and ask for
'Jaws' McMenemie!

Now you may wonder why I've been
browsing in the past like this. Well, the truth
is, this will be my 'Last Call'.

Last Sunday, after twenty-five years, I
preached my last sermon at St Bertie's East
Parish Church. It was an extremely moving
occasion. They only gave me twenty-four
hours to get out of the manse. And what, you
may ask, was the beautiful parting gift from
my loving congregation? Damn all! Not a
sausage! No gold watch; no chromium-plated
toaster – not even a butter dish! And it's not
as if I didn't give them every opportunity at
the service on Sunday. I started off in most
complimentary fashion with hymn 206 –
'GLORIOUS THINGS OF THEE ARE
SPOKEN.' Nothing! Then, I thought, a wee
reminder that I was leaving, so in we went with
hymn 279 – 'THE RADIANT MORN HAS
PASSED AWAY'. Still nothing – so I thought
right, and changed the mood with hymn 122

– 'THE STRIFE IS O'ER, THE BATTLE DONE.'

It was at this point that Mrs Boucher – forever troubled with the wind – let out a rift that nearly unseated the organ – so in we came with an inspired ad lib. Hymn 680 – 'WE HAVE HEARD A JOYFUL SOUND'.

Anyway, about this time I thought they maybe needed a wee nudge about a wee parting gift to their retiring minister, so we quickly swung into Hymn 491 – 'ALMIGHTY FATHER WHO DOST *GIVE*' . . . followed immediately by Hymn 507 – 'I'M NOT AFRAID TO *OWN* – MY LORD.' . . . And that's when they all suddenly stood up and sang Hymn 254 – 'ALL THINGS ARE THINE NO GIFT HAVE WE.'

But then, as it happened, Old Warty Face, the session clerk – ('course he never knew I called him Old Warty Face . . . *DIRECT* . . . but you know now, ya old . . .) anyway, he handed in a bottle of cherry brandy. So I thanked him for his gift of fruit – and the spirit in which it was given.

But, you know I couldn't help thinking back on some of the people I'd met during my 25 years at St Bertie's. There was the lovely Mrs Atkins whose husband died and left her all that money. There was the McIlwhams with fifteen children and bewildered expressions. So little food their canary used to lock his cage from the inside. The lovely Mrs Atkins. Old Baldy Ballantine the organist who wrote that lovely song about a little yellow bird that lost it's way. You may have heard it. 'Auntie Mary had a Canary.' The lovely Mrs Atkins. Old Tam Caldwell who grew the BIGGEST MARROW IN THE PARISH and one night during a severe and unexpected frost, he was staggering home blind drunk after Bible class, took a short cut through his allotment, tripped over his runner beans and fell spreadeagled – and that's where we found him in the morning – frozen to the marrow.

But now it's all over. Tomorrow I leave for Mallorca with the lovely Mrs Atkins and to all my . . . 'friends' and colleagues at St. Bertie's

East Parish Church I would just like to say –
God bless you – and . . . *he blows a huge
raspberry.*

9

LUCKY WHITE HEATHER

Rev I.M. Jolly

(Very gloomily): Hullo! What sort of day have you had? Has it been a good day? Has it been happy for you? Did something wonderful happen to you – like your train coming in on time – or your electricity bill being less than you thought it would be? (I'm joking, of course!) No. Far more important than 'what sort of day have YOU had' . . . is the question – 'what have you done to make this day better for others?' I believe, you see, that it is more important to make someone else happy than to be happy yourself. It is essential when you are having a good day to share the joy of it with your fellow men.

For myself, I have had a helluva day! In fact,

the whole week has been something of a pain in the arm for me. I think, perhaps, I pulled a muscle the other night when conducting the choir. The choir! That is a laugh. Two old men and a snotty-nosed youth from an approved school. We foster him, you know. It's like living with a piranha fish. Then on Monday I had to clear up the whole area in front of the pulpit. With shovel and wheelbarrow I laboured long. All because Mrs McCandlish, the coalman's wife, had this remarkable idea of sitting on top of her husband's Clydesdale and doing the Sermon on the Mount. Well, whether the horse was embarrassed or frightened, I don't know, but . . .

Anyway, all that carry-on with the shovel and the wheelbarrow put my back out, and between that and my arm, I was up all night. The pain was excruciating. I sprayed it with liniment, but there was just no improvement. You know that awful way when it just doesn't matter how you lie – you just cannot get relief. I tried this way and that. Eventually I ended up sort of kneeling with one arm up the chimney and the other under the pillow. My head in the bedside cabinet – one leg outside the bed and the other across my good lady. She being a decisive woman and in some doubt as to my intentions, rose up and belted me one.

I think it was at this point the dog was sick. Probably the smell of the liniment. Not that I mind the poor beast bringing up his dinner – it's just that, of course, he would sleep at MY side. By the time I got that lot cleaned up it was time to rise and shine . . . when suddenly there was a ring at the front door and when I opened it – there was this sweet little girl selling lucky white heather. My case comes up next Tuesday.

Goodnight.

10

WISH YOU WERE HERE

Rev I.M. Jolly

Hullo! It was with a great feeling of joy that I accepted the invitation to come along and have one of our uplifting little chats together. As you can see, I'm quite overcome. Indeed, I'm finding it quite difficult to speak because of the emotions which are surging within me.

After my last broadcast – at least I understood from the BBC, that it was to be my last broadcast – I received hundreds of letters from you. When I say hundreds, there was, in fact, about twenty or thirty . . . Well, to be absolutely honest there was this postcard from Ayr – it showed the cemetery at the Auld Kirk and bore the legend – 'Wish you were here!' I suppose it was meant to be a joke. I didn't laugh – although, as most of you know, I have a pretty lively sense of humour.

However, I gather that my talk last time had some beneficial effect. Many of you decided, after listening to me, that your own lives were not nearly so bad as you had been thinking.

Of course, this is our function in life. To lighten the load, if we can, of our fellow humans. A cheery word here – a smile of encouragement there. And I think it's important not to give people the impression that I'm any different from them. I mean I often go into a pub and have a drink just as if I was normal.

I must admit that one of my greatest help-mates is my wife Ephesia. I just don't know what I would do without her – even if I got the chance. She accompanies me everywhere I go. It's either that or having to kiss her goodbye. But I'm sure you'll agree that it is wonderful to be blessed with a good life partner, and I can truly say that our marriage was made in Heaven. It's not so good down here, but it's nice to have something to look forward to.

Of course there are times when, in spite of a cheery disposition and personal warmth, you feel somewhat inadequate. For instance, a woman phoned me the other day saying she was going to do away with herself. So, of course, I rushed round, and there she was, standing on a chair in the middle of the sitting-room with the flex from the centre light round her neck.

You could see she was upset. But – oh, could I get a word in? She stood there shouting abuse, cursing and swearing – just wouldn't listen to anything I had to say. So I just kicked the chair away.

And now a prayer. Oh, God . . . !

11

KEEP SMILING

Rev J.M. Jolly

Hullo! Do you ever get the feeling that life's just one great disaster area? That, some mornings, you just shouldn't get up? That everybody and everything is against you? . . . So do I! Yes, it'll maybe surprise you to know that I'm not always the chirpy happy-go-lucky chap I make myself out to be.

So this is my message to all of you. KEEP SMILING! It's worth remembering what Plato once said . . . 'QUAE FERUNT VITIA, MORES SUNT.' I don't know what it means, but it's worth remembering.

Of course, as I've said before, I am lucky to have a very dear wife. I don't think you could get a dearer wife! Ephesia. She's a remarkable woman. On Monday she just made up her mind, went into the hairdresser and had her hair cut off. She came out looking like a new man. Mind you I have to admit she's always had a sort of masculine appearance.

I think it's the moustache. Indeed, for the first three years of our courtship I was convinced I was still going out with the boys. But like me, she has this great ability to see the funny side of things. When I told her, for instance, that old Mr McCorkindale had died intestate, she remarked that it was probably because he hadn't had enough roughage in his diet! I have to laugh. It's as much as my life's worth.

Not that there was much to laugh about last week. The church concert wasn't exactly what you'd describe as the acme of show business. To start with, the grand piano fell off the stage and became an upright. Then part of the curtain came away during Mrs McCandlish's solo. I would have come away myself if I'd had the chance. Although I was quite glad I stayed

when almost immediately a piece of scenery fell
and tore off the front part of her dress. It was
pure irony that it happened while she was
singing 'These Are My Mountains'.

Still, we made a clear profit of ninety-six pee
which has been put to the Roof Repair Fund
– and that means we can buy another slate.

Then on Sunday, old Mr Pettigrew had a
disaster with his organ. It's an antiquated old
thing that should have gone on the rubbish
heap long ago. Not unlike old Mr Pettigrew.
Honestly, the time that's spent between hymns
while he fiddles with his feet and changes his
combinations . . . ! Anyway, it's old Mrs
Agnew that pumps for him. And it's a generally
accepted fact that there's just nobody that can
pump like Mrs Agnew. She's quite the strongest
pumper we've ever had in the church. But then
she's been pumping on and off for over sixty
years and it is obviously something that comes
natural to her. Oh, people come from far
and near when word gets round that Mrs
Agnew is going to pump. Believe me, when

Mrs Agnew pumps, you know somebody has pumped! However, most unfortunately, last Sunday during Evensong Mrs Agnew was pumping away with her usual zeal when, quite suddenly, her lever broke. Just came away in her hand. Right in the middle of a pump. Not that it bothered Mrs Agnew, but it certainly put the wind up old Mr Pettigrew. So, the moral is that wherever you be – let your sense of humour prevail. Goodnight.

12

MY WIFE, EPHESIA

Rev J.M. Jolly

Hullo! Well – that's another year gone! Any minute now we'll be facing a new, vigorous, thrilling, challenging, dynamic era. I don't know about you, but I'm incredibly moved. I can hardly speak for the turbulent emotions which are surging through my body – if you'll pardon the expression. I just don't know when I've been so excited. My wife, Ephesia, says she can't remember either.

And soon the bells'll be ringing out their joyous message of hope and cheer and goodwill-towards-men and love-thy-neighbour, and all the ships too, on the Clyde, will set their sirens screaming and – what with the bells and the screaming sirens – a good New Year will be upon us. Not to mention a good-going earache as well.

And what sort of year have you had? Has it been a good year? Has it been happy? Has it been successful? But enough of this waggishness!

For myself, I try not to think of this past year as having been an uphill struggle – hardship, suffering, gloom and despondency. I like to think of it more as sheer misery.

Mind you, it has been an interesting year in many ways. In the last twelve months I have been to no less than a hundred-and-forty-seven funerals! Not in an official capacity, you understand. It's really just a wee kind of hobby of mine. And, of course, if it's a morning 'do' it always saves you making your own lunch. Ephesia enjoys them, too, for she likes meeting people. Even if it is too late!

In the spring, Ephesia, forever seeking ways to harness her great energy, started up a soup kitchen for down-and-outs. Unfortunately, the only people who kept turning up were her relatives. But then, in no time, word got round – and my family turned up as well.

Later in the year she came with me when I went to London as a member of a working party from the Motherwell Municipal Home for Maladjusted Ministers. Or as we call it – Mmhmm!

Ephesia was particularly interested in the problems of vice in the big city and during her research in Soho, invited a number of us to view a typical pornographic film. Well, I mean, honestly – four letter words, nudity, violence and sleazy sex!!!

I enjoyed it!

And to put your minds at rest, I can assure you that it's something that quickly loses its appeal. I mean, I saw it fourteen times and I know.

Anyway 1980 is now in the past.

We must look to the future and Ephesia and I do wish you whatever's coming to you in 1981. And to you, if you live alone – mind your back!

But I leave you with this thought. Look to your fellow man, your neighbour. Love him, and trust him – he will not fail you – and together you will go forward to a bigger, better, BRIGHTER FUTURE than ever before. And if you can believe that . . . YOU CAN BELIEVE ANYTHING!

13

HIGHLIGHTS
OF MY YEAR

Rev I.M. Jolly

Hullo! You're probably all sitting out there saying, 'What's HE got to be so cheery about?' Well, don't be taken in by this air of devil-may-care abandon. Like many of you, I'm sure, I often sit here and suffer. I got some ointment for it, but . . .

Anyway, what sort of year have you had? Has it been a good year? Has it been full of happiness, excitement . . . joy!

That must be the biggest laugh since the Tay Bridge Disaster. On the other hand – speaking personally – I've had a helluva year.

To start with, we had a terrible accident in the church choir. Old Mr Jamieson, who sings soprano for us, tried to reach a top C and burst his braces.

Then Mrs Pattison, our church organist, got a wee bit over-excited playing a complicated Bach fugue and ruined her combinations. But there was a lesson in all of this. It brought home to me what my old professor used to say.

'Don't waste time and energy thinking about yourself, and getting depressed,' he said. 'Look around you. Think of others. And get depressed about them!'

I don't know about you, but I hate New Year. Isn't it funny how you always look back and think of something you wish you hadn't done. Speaking of the wife – Ephesia wasn't quite herself for a while. It was great while it lasted, but . . .

Actually, I think it started with the World Cup. She enjoyed it tremendously, but she found it pretty tiring. She was playing right-back for Poland.

Of course I can always tell when Ephesia's under a lot of pressure – being so close to her.

Oh, there are lots of signs. Just little things like coming home and finding my slippers waiting for me – in the fridge.

Mind you, there was a highlight to the year. The Womens' Guild decided to have their Church outing in Mallorca this year. Old Clem Sinclair had managed to get what he called 'a very good deal' from Fly-by-Night Tours. £35-a-head and find your own way to Barcelona.

Well, if you'd seen the plane. We'd to give it a shove down the hill to get it started. Actually, the trip wouldn't have been so bad if it hadn't been for these two kids running up and down the aisle laughing and shouting. Oh, I soon put a stop to that. I just opened a door and told them to play outside.

Oh, if you could have heard the mother. What she didn't call me! That was alright too, though. She went out to look for them.

The Hotel Basura, as it was called, was a huge place. Over four hundred beds. Unfortunately, they were all in the one room.

But there was plenty to do and I could see that Ephesia was beginning to relax. In fact, one day she came down to the beach topless! I must say I didn't approve and said so. So she put the wig back on. There was a lovely three-and-a-half hole golf course there, too. I hadn't played golf for years and suggested to Ephesia that we play a round. But she had a headache as usual. Anyway, now she's back refreshed and thrown herself into her social work again among the misfits of society, the bewildered and feeble-minded. Or as I call them – her family.

And that's the old year gone. I'm sure 1983'll be much better. Wouldn't bank on it, mind you. But, you know, I always remember what my dear old father used to say to me. 'Angela,' he would say. (He'd a terrible memory for names. At least that's what he said!) 'Angela,' he would say, 'no matter what muck life throws at you, smile. Keep smiling because, let's face it, things could be worse.' And that's what I did. I just smiled. And you

know, my dear old father was right.
Things are a bloody sight worse.

14

GOINGS-ON IN THE PARISH

Rev I.M. Jolly

Hullo! Well, that's another year we've managed to put in.

(Jolly blows a party squeaker.)

I'll bet that surprised you . . . It certainly put the wind up ME! I suppose I get a wee bit skittish at this time of the year. I've really got to keep a tight rein on myself or I'd do something outrageous like rushing into the BBC and shouting 'SCOTTISH TELE-VISION!!!!' And it's not that I'm all that happy about it being New Year – it's just that I'm that damn glad to see the back of the OLD one.

So here we are – trembling at the gate of 1984. A year so vividly described by George

Orwell in his book called – er – in that book
he wrote. And what nonsense it contained.
What a load of crass stupidity.

'Big Brother's watching you!'

Big SISTER maybe – but BIG Brother?!

I don't know about you, but looking
forward to another year with its new challenges and problems always gives me a feeling of
– what's the word? . . . NAUSEA!

Anyway, what sort of festeri – festive season
have you had? Did you have a happy time or
did your relations come to visit you? Did you
get just what you've always wanted for
Christmas? Did your tree stay up? Did your
fairy lights work?

But enough of this pawkiness!

Our own season was something of a mixed
bag. And speaking of the wife, Ephesia invited
her entire family this year and cooked
Christmas dinner for them. I really had to hand
it to her. After all these years she got her own
back at one fell swoop!

There have been all SORTS of goings-on in

the parish. Our local flasher came to see me in a very distressed state. Apparently he'd developed a terrible inferiority complex 'cos people kept laughing at him.

Our organist, old Mr Bampot, fell off his organ in September – fractured his treble and damaged his combinations. And he was no sooner out and about again when he was struck by a second tragedy. It seems he'd received two Christmas presents which were identical, only different. One was a set of that waterproof underwear. I don't know *what* you call them, but it's got something to do with what old people wear on the continent. And the other present was a set of THERMAL underwear that were so old-fashioned you had to plug them into the mains.

Well, it seems he was wearing them BOTH at the Watch Night Service and – well, we don't really know WHAT happened – I think maybe he got a wee bit excited during Handel's 'Water Music' . . . anyway. There was this tremendous flash, and the next thing we knew we were all standing there singing 'HE IS GONE BEYOND THE SKIES'. Unaccompanied. So it's not been a happy year for us. Especially when we remember that we'd not long had the organ overhauled. But now – a prayer. Oh, Lord, teach us to have chastity and restraint. But not just yet!

Goodnight.

15

MORE EMBARRASSMENTS

Rev I.M. Jolly

Hullo!

Well, here I am again, positively flushed with const– anticipation at the thought of us prancing merrily, hand-in-hand, through the gates of 1985.

What delights are in store for us?

Meeting Jimmy Saville on the 5.35 to Edinburgh? Meeting Jimmy Saville ANY-WHERE? But enough of this couthy, home-spun humour.

I've had one or two letters since I last spoke to you. There was an interesting one from a woman who couldn't make up her mind if she should seek a separation – and if she did, would her husband have to support her, and could I offer some sort of uplift.

My good lady, Ephesia, has one of these brassieres. Not a small size, I must admit. In fact, it's not the first time she's forgotten her shopping basket and brought home a couple of stone of potatoes in it. Notwithstanding – and it WASN'T with standing – Ephesia was awful keen that we should try a holiday in a nudist camp last summer.

I must say I didn't enjoy it all that much. You get awful bored just hanging about all day.

It was fun queuing for the barbecue, mind you, but then I've always enjoyed meeting people.

And, of course, nothing would do but my dear wife had to enter for the Glasgow Marathon. She was doing quite well, too. Head down, pushing herself along like a hippopotamus in labour. When suddenly she experienced a head-on collision with a double-decker bus.

The bus was a write-off – and Ephesia was knocked more unconscious than usual at my feet. Well, the people immediately crowded round us. It was awfully embarrassing for her. Not one of the men would volunteer to give her the kiss of life. Not even when I offered them money. By this time she had lost her jumper. It had flown off into a field and some people were using it as a refreshment tent. Then the bus driver rushed up and looked down at her lying there topless.

'Oh,' he says, 'that's terrible.' Well, I couldn't argue with that. I mean I've ALWAYS thought so. 'What do you think we ought to do,' he says, and some wag in the crowd said, 'If I were you, mate,' he said, 'Ah would treat it as a double roundabout.'

But our really testing time was just the other week when we held our Winter Fair. It wasn't exactly a howling success . . . more what you might call an unmitigated disaster.

Since we're a mining community we duly elected our Miss Coalface of 1984. It was supposed to be big Annie McPartland but she got pregnant and couldn't get into the frock.

So we had to rope in Mrs McCandlish, the coalman's wife. Well, I know I shouldn't say it, but I can't stand that woman. Oh, she gives me a pain in the armpit. Talk, talk, talk – always talking. In fact, she reminds me of one of these Venus's flytraps. The only time her mouth's shut is when there's food in it.

The next thing that happened is that old Mr Bampot, who's ninety-three and pretty frail, entered the grass-cutting competition with a Flymo.

He was shot down over Pittenweem.

The final catastrophe was the Dinner Dance later that night. We had the dance alright – but nobody had remembered to organise the dinner. So, Mrs McCandlish had to rush down to the Chinese carry-out for fifty-nine portions of haddock and chips.

Well, we weren't sure WHAT happened. Apparently the wee Chinaman said something she took exception to. She started battering the poor man over the head with her umbrella. Fortunately, she desisted when someone explained that what the Chinaman had actually said was 'FISH OFF'. Oh, there was worse to come. This raving lunatic rushed into the shop and started belting the McCandlish woman with a black pudding. Honestly, can you imagine such rampant idiocy, such blundering stupidity. My lawyer says I should plead diminished responsibility.

Goodnight.

16

HOPE IN OUR HEARTS

Rev J.M. Jolly

Hullo! 'And the wind rose. And Simon was much troubled. And they chided him saying, "Why art thou so troubled with the wind?" And he was made to sit at the far end of the boat.'

Then again . . .

'And it came to pass that he travelled for six days and six nights and came unto the house of Mary, but lo, she was not in. Whereupon he left a note unto her saying, "I pulled thy bell and ye answered me not. I knocked thy knocker and ye answered me not. Wherefore I keeked through thy window and saw thee hiding under the bed. And I felt angry and betrayed. So I kicked thy ox and thy ass and all that was thine. And emptied thy dustbin over thy lawn."'

These are just two of the texts I'd like to talk to you about this Hogmanay. We set off along the road with hope in our hearts and bells ringing in our ears. A bevvy in one hand and a packet of crisps in the other. But, you see, we forget that we're all subject to the call – er – to the forces of nature! All these pressures – pleasures – have to be paid for. And if we eat only of the rich food and drink only of the red wine, what happens? We find ourselves throwing up down the toilet of life. What you put into it, is truly what you get out of it!

The important thing to remember is that we can't be happy all the time. Look at me, for instance. I'm not always like this. Sometimes I'm quite miserable.

I used to visit an old lady. Let's call her Hilda. 'Cos that's her name. Hilda Harrison. Eighty-four, and a brighter, cheerier old dear you couldn't meet in a month of Saturdays. She's Jewish! But she never let's anything get her down. Always smiling, always laughing, always ready with a cheery word. Makes ye sick! And she hadn't had her troubles to find.

Her husband hadn't worked from the day they were married. Although, to his credit, he did go to nightschool to learn a trade, so he'd know what kind of job he was out of. I just don't know how they'd have lived if Hilda hadn't owned a chain of supermarkets.

Anyway, about twenty years ago, he left her and went off with another woman. Hilda wouldn't have minded, but it was the marriage guidance counsellor.

Then her grandson got a job with the Railway Police. What a tragedy. They took him down to Central Station one very dark night and told him, 'Your job is to patrol from the booking office to that red light over there'. Never seen again. The red light was on a train going to Cornwall!

Then, finally, there was her grand-daughter. I was asked to perform the marriage ceremony in October there – and six weeks later she had a baby boy. Can you imagine that? Nearly eight months premature!

Which brings me to my opening reference to Simon.

So many people in our society are made to sit at the end of the boat.

Here's a letter I have received from a Mr Archibald McClumpha.

Dear Mr Jolly,

I am 27 years old, have been married four times, and I have 13 children. I don't go out much. Last month my wife left me, took all the children – but left her mother. I recently lost my job at the Golden Future Employment Agency, and had to pay them redundancy. Since then, the electricity and telephone have been cut off, and there's no food in the house. And to top it all, last night the budgie died without saying goodbye. That was the last straw. I am desperate. Mr Jolly – please help me. To be honest if I had the money, I would take the bus to Erskine Bridge and jump off.

Well, of course, I couldn't ignore such a heart-rending plea from this poor man. So I sent him his bus fare!

Goodnight.

17

DECK OF CARDS

Rev I.M. Jolly

Hullo! And it came to pass that the skies darkened, the trees bent in the wind, the heavens opened and it rained for forty days and forty nights. So much for the summer!

Typically, we'll all be looking to next year, and hoping things will be better. But at this time of year we should also take a look behind us, keeping alive some of our HAPPIEST memories. For example, I can remember the day I first met my wife Ephesia.

That's maybe not the best example, but still . . . I had been officiating at a Christmas wedding in Falkirk. It was a mixed marriage. She came from Edinburgh and he came from Glasgow. Anyway, during the reception, I met

Ephesia just outside the ladies toilet. (She was going in just as I was coming out.) And suddenly she held a small bunch of mistletoe over my head and kissed me. Of course, I kissed her back. (I certainly wasn't going to kiss her face!) But it's amazing to think that we've been inseparable ever since. Like chewing gum on the sole of life.

That was also the year I started making my hospital visits. Going round the wards, giving uplifting, cheery little talks to the elderly patients. How often I've had cause to be grateful that I went in time. So many of them passed away just after I'd been there.

And it was at New Year one year when I was returning home by train that a fight broke out in my compartment. Three young men quarrelled over a game of poker, and suddenly one of them began driving his knee again and again into the groin of an innocent passenger. I had to intervene. After all, it was MY groin!

But I took the opportunity of explaining how a deck of cards can offer us a great deal of spiritual insight. For example, when I see the ace, two and three, I think of young Jason McClumpha who was caught moonlighting and drawing his dole at the same time.

He was called before three DHSS inspectors who asked him his name. 'Joseph,' he replied cheekily.

'What's your wife's name?' they asked him.

'Mary,' he replied.

'Where do you live?' they asked him.

'Nazareth,' he said.

'Well, Joseph', they said, 'Just you go home to Nazareth and tell Mary that THE THREE WISE MEN have stopped your burroo money!'

The four reminds me of the number of people in the congregation at last week's Evening Service. The five and six the fifty-six pence we took in the collection.

When I see the seven, eight and nine, I remember that was the number of the hotel bedroom where I spent my honeymoon. It was absolute bliss, even though Ephesia had had to stay at home with a headache. I was young then and quite daring. I asked the chambermaid to bring me early morning tea – at four o'clock! I was still awake when the knock came and a PORTER brought in the tea. 'Where's the chambermaid?' I asked, somewhat disappointed. 'I don't know, sir,' he replied. 'But the teapot's made in Birmingham.'

The ten makes me think of the choir – Ten Wise Virgins. I've never believed in Foolish Virgins – they always seemed a contradiction in terms. And the Jack, of course, old Jack Bampot, organist and choirmaster whose renderings on the organ get more and more like 'Name That Tune'.

The Queen is, of course, my good lady Ephesia who's been on a diet for six weeks and all she's lost is her temper. However, this time she has a real incentive to get her weight down as she's been offered the title role in the Dramatic Society's stage version of *Moby Dick*.

And finally, there is the King which I see as

my father who taught me the real meaning of TRUTH. My father worked in the mill at Luncarty, and we lived in a little cottage which had an outside toilet about a hundred yards away, standing at the edge of the river. One day our toilet was found upside down in the water. My father called me to him. 'Agnes, I am going to ask you a question, but before I do I want you to remember the story of George Washington who cut down his father's favourite cherry tree and who, when asked, declared, "I cannot tell a lie, father. It was I who cut down the cherry tree." And his father REWARDED him. Now,' said my father. 'What can you tell me about the toilet?'

'I cannot tell a lie,' I cried. 'I pushed the toilet into the river!'

Well, he nearly murdered me! I've never had such a thrashing in my life.

I cried out in despair. 'But, Father,' I said, 'You told me that George Washington said, "I cut down the cherry tree," and his father REWARDED HIM!'

'I know,' said my father, 'but George Washington's father was NOT SITTING IN THE CHERRY TREE when it was cut down!'

Goodnight.

18

THE PARABLE OF MISADVENTURE

Rev I.M. Jolly

Hullo!

Death, disaster, famine, disease – the Poll Tax! I suppose some of you sometimes think that life's not worth living.

Oh, so do I.

What a Christmas! For one thing we couldn't find the fairy lights. Searched everywhere.

Then eventually we discovered the dog had taken them into his kennel. He's just a wee dog with legs like a fox terrier and a face like a boxer. A wee bit like Barry McGuigan. But there, in his kennel, he had the fairy lights all strung out in neat little loops. Ephesia was very impressed. 'There you are,' she said to me. 'The bloomin' dog's a damn sight cleverer than YOU are.' I said, 'He's not *so* clever. HE can't make them work either!'

Then the fairy fell off the top of the Christmas tree. Though what he was doing there in the first place, I don't know.

Then I christened a child THINGBY McCLAFFERTY. THINGBY! The mother couldn't remember what she'd decided to call her. When I took the babe in my arms I said to the mother, 'But this child's head is already wet.' She said, 'I know. You're holding it upside down.' I must say I had wondered about the enormous grin on its face.

And this year we had decided to put up an illuminated Christmas message above the church door. Unfortunately Mercedes McClumpha, the session secretary who would have to make the arrangements wasn't at that meeting. So . . . I went round to her house and popped a note through her letter box giving the text of the message AND the dimensions of the sign. Apparently she collapsed in a dead heap when she read the note, for it said, 'UNTO US A CHILD IS BORN. EIGHT FEET HIGH AND FIVE FEET WIDE!'

So, it was all a time of frustration and disappointment for me, but I long ago learned to laugh off such irritations. It rather reminded me of that other ancient parable of misadventure which you may remember.

And lo, there were ten vestal virgins. Five were wise virgins and five were foolish virgins. And the five wise virgins were elderly and irritable for they had been wise for many years, and it was getting on their wick.

And it came to pass that these ten virgins were called upon to attend a bridal feast with their lamps. And during the celebrations the five foolish virgins partook of the good wine in abundance and one by one their lamps went out.

And when they awoke they said unto the wise virgins, 'Give us of your oil that we might replenish our lamps,' and the wise virgins spake unto them saying, 'Get thyselves knotted. Go into the market place, get thyselves a trolley, and purchase that which you need.' So the five foolish virgins set off, but came unto the wrong market place. And they spake unto a Sadducee who was there, saying, 'We are five foolish virgins who need our wicks trimmed and our oil replenishing.' 'Go ye to yonder house,' replied the Sadducee. 'Knock thrice upon the door and ask for Obadiah.' The foolish virgins did as they were bidden and approaching a small door knocked three times. Whereupon it was opened unto them and they spake saying, 'We are five foolish virgins.' 'Thou hast come to the right place,' said Obadiah. And, lo, they entered – otherwise they would have bumped their heads on the door. And having no light, they had to sit in the dark with the boys. Which was very foolish, for though they kept their hands on their lamps, they were soon well oiled.

And it came to pass that when the five foolish virgins returned to the feast they spake unto the wise virgins saying, 'Rejoice, sisters, for we are not the foolish virgins that ye knew. For not only have we lost our FOOLISHNESS, but we have lost our lamps as well.'

Goodnight.

19

COOL IMAGE AND CHANGE OF GEAR

Rev I.M. Jolly

Lighting comes up and the familiar face of Jolly is seen. The clothing is different, however. In place of the well-known grey flannel there is a sleeveless, denim bomber jacket, an enormous medallion and chain, a belt with an oversize buckle, bracelets on his arm and rings on his fingers, and of course his clerical smock and white collar. There is the usual shuddering intake of breath then:

Hi! *(He tries to snap his fingers, but doesn't quite succeed.)*

You'll maybe notice a slight difference in my appearance. Magic, eh? It was Ephesia who suggested it. She's my live-in-lover! By marriage! She said I should get my act together – put up a cool image and change the gear. Apparently I've been in reverse for years. So here I am 'beatin'-the-streets in my clean jeans and havin' a few bevvies-with-the-heavies!'

I feel a right pillock!

Though, to be honest, I would have to laugh – if I could get my face to work that way. I attended the Christmas social dressed like this. It was really gravy. Groovy. Did the hokey-cokey, shook it all about and got a hernia. Even pulled a wee cracker. It went 'Bang!' I asked a young chick if she thought my outfit was 'pure dead brilliant,' and she said, well, she wasn't sure about the brilliant!

Apart from that, Christmas has been something of a mixed bag. And speaking of Ephesia, she gave me my usual present of two large, gift-wrapped bottles of Sloan's Liniment, And I gave her her usual catering-size of Germolene. Her feet have given her trouble for years. Tho' not as much as they've given me!

In fact it's not been too good a time health-wise. We put in one of these orthopaedic beds you get for a sore back; and I must say it was remarkable; inside a fortnight we both had one.

And, sadly, we lost two of our most worthy church members this year. Elijah Snash, he was only sixty-three, died of amnesia. He was driving happily along the M8 on his motorbike when somebody passed him going so fast he thought he had stopped. So he got off to see what was wrong.

Then there was the rather sad case of two elderly parishoners – let's call them Betty and Willie – 'cos that was their names. Well, they were in their late seventies and they met at the local disco. And after only two or three weeks they decided they wanted to marry and came to me for the pre-nuptial chat. Which I was quite happy to do, although I thought I would leave out the 'joys of sex' bit, for it was common knowledge that Willie had trouble getting up the stairs, never mind . . . However, Betty insisted on knowing EVERYTHING about, as she put it, S-E-C-K-S. And I thought, my God, if they can't even SPELL it . . . Anyway, I explained that it was meant to be a JOYFUL thing. Certainly it made Ephesia laugh!

Not that we have any problems, I mean there was ONE time . . . No, I tell a lie, there were TWO times . . . And I'm pretty sure there would have been THREE if she hadn't got that goldfish. Anyway, as I was saying, I was explaining as best I could to Willie and Betty. A few practical tips, a hastily drawn diagram and, of course, a prayer.

Well, sadly, Willie didn't survive the honeymoon. Apparently the preliminaries had gone well – the deodorant, the cocoa, the dentures et cetera, but unfortunately, at a somewhat crucial stage they'd got the diagram upside down and, well, Betty's a good eighteen stones.

Goodnight.

20

I AM JOKING,
OF COURSE

Rev I.M. Jolly

Hullo!

My name is Jolly. Spelt M-O-R-B-I-D. So what sort of Christmas have you had? Was Santa good to you? Is your house fair bulging with video recorders and twelve-year-old malts and Swiss watches?

I got a sock!

I bet you thought I was going to say *(pointing to his chin)* 'Right here!' *(Holding his ear.)* It was right here! I am joking, of course. I really did get just the one sock. It might have been two, but Ephesia got fed up. She hates knitting. She says it's not a fit occupation for the Bearsden Ladies Mud-Wrestling Champion.

Still, it's the thought that counts, and a sock is very handy for . . . keeping one of your feet in. And, as Ephesia says, now she's got a good idea what to give me for my birthday.

It's been a funny sort of year. Not that I can remember actually LAUGHING.

'Course, there was all that excitement when old Mr Bampot was presented to the Queen. I think the Queen was a bit startled herself – she usually just gets flowers. Then, in June, Ephesia 'discovered her body'! Thank God I was out at the time. I think it had something to do with the fact that she'd had a wee operation earlier on. She was having the telephone removed from her ear. Anyway, this diet only lasted a couple of days. What with the bran flakes and the fish oil and the baked beans and jogging in hot weather, I was sure she was going to blow another hole in the ozone layer. I mean, it has to be said there were times when she wasn't exactly what you could call OZONE-FRIENDLY. But as she said herself 'it's an ill-wind'.

Funny how 'green-conscious' we've all become this year. Even Rangers! With the environment in mind, I told the story last Sunday of Sodom and Gomorrah. How difficult it is even to read. Especially that bit about all the drinking and sex and fornication and orgies with naked women. *(He drinks a glass of water.)* Anyway, it came to pass that Shem begat Arphaxad, Arphaxad begat Salah, Salah begat Eber, Eber begat Peleg, Peleg begat Jason, Jason begat Kylie, Kylie begat Fiona, Fiona begat Senga, Senga begat Mrs McClumpha, Mrs McClumpha begat Deirdre and MR McClumpha said it wasnie his – and begat Jeremy by someone else entirely.

And the High Priest of the city came to King Bera and said, 'the people want the city to be given a name, what thinkest thou?' 'Oh, sod 'em,' said the King. So Sodom it was. And it came to pass that Lot was sitting outside the gates one day singing 'How Are Things in Sodom and Gomorrah', when two strangers approached him. And Lot bowed low before them with his head toward the ground – mainly because it's extremely difficult to do the other way. 'Come into my house,' said Lot. 'Have something to eat, and wash your feet. PLEASE!' And they said to him 'The city is to be demolished to make way for a motorway. We shall take your family. Go thou and take your ox and your ass and everything that is yours out of the city.' And Lot said, 'I don't have an ox.' 'Well,' they said, 'we'll take your family. Just you get your ass out of here.' And they said, 'As you go away from the city, do not look back lest you see how we do this and go into the demolition business for yourself.' But as they left, Lot's wife turned and looked back, and was turned into a pillar of salt. And Lot made a packet out of it.

It's a dreadful story. It's so difficult to understand what it was like. Especially that bit about all the drinking and sex and fornication and orgies with naked women.

(A slight smile as he lets it sink in.)

I think I'll maybe just have to go home and read that bit again.

21

PARISH FESTIVITIES

Rev I.M. Jolly

Hullo! Well, what sort of Year of Culture have you had? Did you manage to get in to see Frank Sinatra? I'm not asking if you bought tickets – I'm asking if you managed to get in to see Frank Sinatra. Ephesia wanted to see Pavarotti AND Frank Sinatra, so we had to get a bridging loan!

We, of course, had our OWN Parish of Culture Festivities. They have to rank as the most depressing series of monumental cock-ups ever!

Really quite cheered me up. Old Mrs Abernethy opened her house to the public, and everybody living upwind of it got a rent rebate! I'm not saying the house is dirty, but I happen to know that the cockroaches have formed their own Housing Association! Mind you, she's a poor old soul. Six months ago I discovered she had no clothes to wear. Imagine having to go about the house every day with no clothes. I've been visiting her regularly!

And just as Glasgow has opened its new concert hall, we opened our new public baths! Originally they had asked a member of Motherwell District Council to perform the opening ceremony, but he was in Japan! On a fact-finding mission apparently – tho' I can't see there being much call for geishas in Motherwell.

To be fair, I gather he hadn't wanted to make the trip, it was just that he couldn't say 'no' – since he doesn't SPEAK Japanese! Which is surprising considering he's been there seven times already.

Anyway, I was asked to open the baths in his stead. We had a glass of tepid Irn Bru in the town hall, then walked to the site, and as we walked down the main street I saw several houses with great notices in their windows saying 'NO POLL TAX HERE', and I thought, 'You're bloody lucky!'

The opening ceremony at the poolside was brief and disastrous. A short prayer, followed by a short selection on the accordion by old Mr Bampot, the church organist. He got into an awful mess with Handel's 'Water Music', but fortunately he had pills for that.

Then Mrs McCandlish, the coalman's wife, appeared in a bright red bikini with a hot flush to match, jumped into the water and sank like a stone. Well, more like a large boulder really.

Completely out of her depth she was. Apparently the council couldn't decide which end should be the SHALLOW end, and had eventually compromised by having it in a separate building two streets away.

In his speech, the Provost paid tribute to the OLD public baths saying that its record for safety was unequalled anywhere. They had been in use, he said, by upwards of a thousand citizens daily for some forty-seven years, and deaths from drowning had never exceeded two-point-three per cent of any one person. And what was even more encouraging, it had nearly always been the same person who had been drowned.

To complete the Gala Opening, a strenuous game of water polo was played between the Barlanark Brawlers and the Stobhill Stranglers. No score will be announced 'til the next-of-kin have been informed.

And now a prayer.

Oh God, gie's a break!

22

SHARING CHRISTMAS GIFTS

Rev I.M. Jolly

Hullo! Here we are again, ready to enter this Temporal Gate we call New Year – eyes on a new and distant horizon – ready to face whatever challenges life has to offer – our heads held high and our hearts full of hope. What a load of *sheer* rubbish!

It's freezin' cold, lashin' with rain, howlin' winds and there's nothin' but Gaelic on the telly. In any case, most of us'll be past caring in a couple of hours.

We had a break-in at the manse on Christmas Eve. There's been quite a few recently and the police have this description of somebody with low self-esteem and whose dreams and ambitions have never been fulfilled.

Sort of half-man, half-Partick Thistle supporter.

What's worrying the neighbours is that if he's disturbed he usually makes mad passionate love to his victims, no matter what sex they are. So Ephesia and I have been taking it in turns to stay in at night. As luck would have it, of course, we were burgled when we were BOTH out. It was awful. All our beautifully gift-wrapped presents were stolen.

Then on Boxing Day the burglar broke in again and brought back the Christmas tree and the fairy lights. Obviously he couldn't get them to work either.

I'd given Ephesia some lovely toilet soap. It was that soap you get for body odour. Marvellous stuff. In less than three days you could smell her a mile away. She gave me some recycled toilet water. She's very conscious of the environment. Well, you have to be when you take up so much if it. She gave me a Black & Decker drill as well, and invited me to bore the wall for a change.

Still, I don't suppose I should let it upset me. So many great religious men have suffered. Probably the greatest martyr to his faith was Job who maintained his faith, in spite of terrible afflictions. His was the biggest family business in the land of UZ. It was known as the local Job Centre. But he lost everything.

Three of his friends came to COMFORT him. You've heard the old saying, 'A Job's Comforter'. I always used to think it was a wee woolly warmer he wore. (A wee woolly warmer. You've got to be careful how you say that.)

Anyway, these friends came. They sat on the ground and wept and threw dust and stoor all over their heads, then they sat for seven days without speaking. And why? 'Cos their mouths were too full of stoor.

Seven days they couldn't speak. *(Pause)* I think I know what to get Ephesia for her birthday.

Goodnight.

23

MY SUNNY
DISPOSITION

Rev I.M. Jolly

Hullo!

Have you ever known so many things to go wrong in the one year? The economy, the coal mines, *Eldorado*!

Worse even than that – they're making a new series of STRATHBLAIR! And the water in our font's frozen over. Last Sunday I was christening babies by throwing ice cubes at them.

It's all terribly depressing. But, of course, I can't ever afford to look miserable. I've always got to make people think I'm bright and gay.

Well BRIGHT anyway!

Actually I've got quite a sunny disposition;

even a certain . . . skittishness at times. You can ask all my friends. He'd tell you! But even with an outgoing personality and super-optimism it must be obvious that things are affecting me. I mean, clearly, I'm not my usual cheery self. The truth is I've been having such awful nightmares. No one has any idea of the horrors I have to face when I go to bed at night. Unless, of course, they've actually MET Ephesia.

What with curlers, the face cleansers and the BODY CREAM! She covers her entire body with the stuff. It's like sleeping next to a monstrous salmon mayonnaise.

Mind you, poor soul, she's had a terrible summer this year. Haven't we all – but you see she's always been a martyr to greenfly and the pesticides always bring her out in a terrible rash. And it makes her terribly grumpy. I mean I was helping to prepare afternoon tea yesterday and I wish you could have heard what she said. All I asked was 'where should I jam the scones!'

I suppose I should make allowances. She

does seem to be suffering from some sort of secondary menopause. It's got so bad, her hot flushes are causing condensation in the bathroom. And she's so impulsive. There's a member of our congregation who's a wee bit like Fergie's financial adviser.

Well, last week his car broke down just outside the manse, so he came to the door and asked if someone would give him a tow. She had her socks and wellies off before you could blink.

Ah well, I suppose we poor men have always been victims of the whims of our women. Look at John the Baptist; he lost his head over Salome. Not SALAMI, incidentally, as old Mr Bampot calls her. I mean salami is a hot foreign dish that . . . Aye, well, right enough!

Interestingly, she married her half-uncle, you know. I've no idea who married his other half.

But the point is I sometimes wonder if Ephesia and me are entirely suited. You see, it's a MIXED marriage. She's from Edinburgh and I'm from Glasgow.

And . . . obviously I don't tell everybody this, but . . . well, we HAD to get married. Her mother said 'over my dead body' and it just seemed too good an opportunity to miss.

Maybe if we'd had children . . . but, as it turned out we couldn't HAVE children. Of course it was MY fault.

I just didn't fancy her!

24

MANY ARE CALLED
BUT FEW ARE CHOSEN

Rev I.M. Jolly

Hullo.

Well, here we are again, eh! Doesn't time fly when you're excruciatingly happy. What a year I've had. Honestly, it's what's-his-name . . . God.

As God's my judge I've had a helluva year. To start with, Ephesia has been telling everybody about her OBE. That's her 'Out of Body Experience'. If only she had the sense not to go back in. You know, she told me she left her body and floated right up to the ceiling and drifted out the window. God, if only I'd been awake at the time, I could have nailed the window shut.

Mind you, I had a strange experience myself. I had a long train journey one time and I was kind of hot and sticky when I got to Glasgow so I booked into one of those massage parlours. And this gorgeous young lady rubbed me all over with baby oil and gave me a lovely massage. And then she leaned right over me and whispered, 'Would you like super sex?' *(Pause)* 'Oh,' I said, 'if it's all the same to you I'll have the soup.'

But the lowest point of this year was a wedding I had to do in September. I'm pretty sure it was a shotgun wedding because the bride looked like she was hiding something up her jukes. I don't think the bridegroom was too happy. When I said, 'Do you take this woman . . .' He said, 'Would you?' The whole thing ended in a riot. It kind of reminded me of the parable of the marriage feast which, as you all know, contains the immortal words: Many are called but few are chosen.

Now, there was a King who lived in – what's

it called – Cumbernauld. He gave a wedding feast for his son, and he sent out slaves to call those who had been invited to the wedding. But they shunned his invitations and made interesting suggestions as to what he might do with them. And the King said, 'Comest, thou mustest. There will be Bovril, and mutton pies, which are even now in the freezer. And, with a DIY wine kit, lo, I have turned water into wine.' And the guests came and they did drink prodigiously of the water which the King had turned into wine, and were soon turning it back into water again.

And when they stuffed their faces with pies and Bovril, a musician played the piano unto them but, lo, some of the pies had not been defrosted and there was wailing and much gnashing of teeth. And one of the guests rose up in anger and threw his pie at the man who was playing the piano. At this the King's wife was outraged and spake unto the servant saying, 'This man has smote my husband's penis. The blame is thine for thou heated not the pies, which is why many were cauld and two were frozen.'

Goodnight.

IS IT THAT TIME ALREADY?
Rikki Fulton

*The bestselling autobiography of
one of Scotland's favourite entertainers*

From his early days compering for the great
dance bands of the 1950s, to classic comedy
performances in *Francie & Josie* and *Scotch
and Wry* and appearances in Hollywood
movies like *Gorky Park*, Rikki Fulton tells
the story of a remarkable life, including his
wartime experiences and being torpedoed
in the Mediterranean. A highly entertaining
account of a distinguished career dedicated
to making people laugh.

RIKKI FULTON'S
THE REV I.M. JOLLY

HOW I FOUND GOD
AND WHY HE WAS HIDING FROM ME

by Tony Roper

*Book One of the hilarious adventures
of Scotland's best-loved minister*

The Reverend I.M. Jolly always has a few
wee problems, but life goes from bad to
worse when he finds out he may soon be
out of a job, thinks his beloved wife
Ephesia is having an affair and that his
parishoners want rid of him. It's enough
to wipe the smile off his face . . .

*Also available on 4-cassette audio tape,
read by Tony Roper*

RIKKI FULTON'S
THE REV I.M. JOLLY

ONE DEITY AT A TIME,
SWEET JESUS

by Tony Roper

*Book Two of the hilarious adventures
of Scotland's best-loved minister*

Just when you thought it was safe to go
to church again, he's back! And now he's
in residence at Balmoral – you can tell
because the flag's at half-mast. But when
Jolly is sent off on a secret mission,
anything could happen. Jolly's back. And
this time he means business.